ALL THE RELEVANT GODS

ROBIN HOUGHTON

Cinnamon Press
INDEPENDENT INNOVATIVE INTERNATIONAL

Published by Cinnamon Press
Meirion House,
Tanygrisiau
Blaenau Ffestiniog,
Gwynedd, LL41 3SU
www.cinnamonpress.com

ISBN: 978-1-910836-95-8
British Library Cataloguing in Publication Data. A CIP record for this book can be obtained from the British Library.

Designed and typeset in Palatino by Cinnamon Press.
Cover design by Jan Fortune.
Printed in Poland
Cinnamon Press is represented in the UK by Inpress Ltd and in Wales by the Welsh Books Council

Acknowledgements

I would like to thank the editors of the following publications, in which many of these poems (or versions of them) first appeared: *Bare Fiction, Envoi, Obsessed with Pipework, Poetry News, Prole, The Poetry Shed* and *The Rialto*. 'Searching for the Police Tower, Orford Ness' won the Poetry Society's 2014 Stanza Competition. 'The houses are coming' and 'Performance' were both nominated for the Forward Prize for best single poem. Thank you to Catherine Smith, Antony Mair and the Hastings Stanza poets, Peter Kenny, Sarah Barnsley and the readers of my blog for their invaluable feedback and encouragement. I am also very grateful for the support I received from New Writing South on its NWS10 scheme.

Contents

All the Relevant Gods

Old ground

So many lakes. I thought I knew this country—
how small that thinking was.
On paper, you show me lakes—and those green places
where flowers grow improbably orange and purple
wildness seeded and stretched in a light pall
over fields bigger than oceans—
then the vineyards and jarrah forests, tall even in 2D.
It's as if a god's waters broke and she never went back
north to where crocodiles lie for weeks in dirt
waiting for the wet—up there in the desert
baubled with placenames I can't pronounce.

We place the map flat, smoothe a creased Pilbara,
follow with fingers the borderline, dishonestly straight.
So few highways they stand out like the heart
head and life lines of your hand. Charted emptiness,
this chimera of land keeps its secrets hidden
like a pouched joey or a man with a stick and a patch
of red earth, looking up at the night, plotting the Pole Star.

Refolding takes time, with each repeat abrasion
risking the loss of one more creek or baobab. I feel it
in my pocket—spring-loaded, ready to bounce away.

The long-haired girls

Take hold of a rope plait, or a bunch,
and you could puppet their heads,
or climb up to a single Rapunzel bed.

They have dreamt up their tresses
over break, between iced laughs
and flicked glances at passing boys.

The prize is long enough to sit on,
its surface dead flat, shinier than glass
ceilings, trussed in a my-little-ponytail.

They examine for split ends daily,
sucking them better, and if they think
you haven't noticed, they'll let it down

before you can blink, shake it all free,
make you look at the sly dip and drop
of curtains across one slow eye.

Sleeping partner

Osmium (Os, atomic number 76, a metal in the platinum group, discovered 1803)

Up from little silver
up the Orinoco
shedding its stench.

Reluctant traveller
not diamond-hard
but almost.

Crystalline. Forget
filigree—
it won't be shaped

or forged.
No plate, no rivers
named for it.

A brittle star
blue in some lights
inking the tip

of my Parker pen.
A shy ingredient
spiralling the grooves

of Bakelite discs
sounding
the twelve bar blues

wearing itself out
with style. Not sapphire
but almost.

Prancer

He came to us over the leads—
a connoisseur of chimneys
and gnarly parapets—

he slid between church roofs,
ground his joints on mossy tiles
while pinnacling.

For the joy of each chase down
he endured the up, chiseling
hoof-holds in slate,

following twizzles of breath
blown from his brothers'
nostrils up front.

He never looked down to the bald
tops of trees or roads asleep,
the town's grotesquerie.

Over the sky parlours, chequers
and marlipins he came, over
the weather vanes,

toeing the gutters and leaping
from gable-ends to bring us each
a tangerine,

a walnut in its knobbly shell,
a book of Aesop's Fables to read
by candlelight.

The houses are coming

from behind hoardings when you're not looking,
trying to live up to the artist's impression.
Down one-way streets the wrong way they slip
to the tune of infill and quotas and backhanders.
They're coming to a field or a muddy ditch near you
seeking out scout huts to flatten or a football pitch
to rotavate, public toilets to macerate. They speak
of small-minded windows, off-plan, open plan,
a seductive flow of concrete footings, drywall,
en suites, third bedrooms the size of a coffin.
The houses spread out from the phantom limbs
of roundabouts, a bloody flowering from brambles,
strong with the tickbox confidence of planners.
No-one cares that the houses share a single heart
and lung, a single thought. Because we want them:
they are what our dogs have been barking for,
what fieldfares and skylarks sing for. They fill up
the untenanted spaces in our minds, they make us
misremember old routes. The houses are coming
and we know they will stub out their cigarettes
on our skin, take everything and keep on taking,
even so, we throw open our front doors, we let them in.

I was expecting a man

I had my voice all ready
the one I get out for lads—

instead I'm silenced
braced for uptalk

and vocal fry—it's as if
I broke open an egg

to find not yolk, but eye—
cartoon-like and rolling

I was sharp with bloke
and up for the banter

left-brain engaged
I was expecting a dog—

the sort that loves
its own stink—food begger

crotch sniffer—not
a little pink kitten

of vowels —it's like it's like
I've got it all wrong

and it must be the way you
spell your name—with

an I instead of *why*
as if to patronise, and yes

I was expecting
a baritone at least

not a soubrette
I was expecting

a lorryload of chummy
orright mates and *yeah not bad*

but now I'm lost
on the end of a phone

about to fill your airspace
with my own she-speak.

Handmade in Guangzhou

Past an open door big enough to drive in,
a soup of steamed up figures just visible inside,
angled shouts over the hatcheting of hung meat.

Up a wide staircase: lino into whitewash as we climb
back-lit by metal framed windows, a token logo
greets us— hand painted, not quite the right pantone.

Long tables in the machine room, ribbons of women
poised at their work, pressed together in pairs, bowed
as if praying to the western god of sports & leisure.

We are the tall, pale Americans—curiosities—stalked
by stares. I cannot make eye contact, though I try.
Instead I catch only the tops of bent-over heads.

In a glass-walled cell, our forearms lean on drawings,
add *two mils* here, re-form midsole contours, laugh
at our own jokes. Next door the still life of a break:

rows of workers asleep at their stations, and us
having boxed pizza and Coke brought in, still arguing
over mesh, the heat, sock liner thicknesses.

Evening brings a flickering from the window: outside
and below, sitting in the dust a crowd out-gazes us. *Top Gun*
in projection, our faces a small flaw on the big screen.

All the relevant gods

Sagra's office walls flare chilli and lime.
To enter is to firewalk:
my dry skin reddens.

If Sagra's mood is aflame, she's up
and at me, black flap of hair shake-shaking—
Sagra is whiplash of Carnival,
staccato rage and/or joy—
more shout than song,
gravelling my face with Spanish expletives.

I'm as passive as the laptops around us.
But Sagra is tall,
higher than the jungle canopy
up on a Mayan pyramid
high on chocolate with Itzamna and Ixchel.
She breathes rainforest and speaks sky,
more miraculous than the giant hummingbird
drawn in the desert grit
                                        and I know this:
every morning
her sly lump of an English boyfriend
must grope out of Sagra's fragrant bed,
examine the cold play of mirror
and thank all the relevant gods
for whatever it is she sees in him.

She discovered the internet

Between the red meeting room and the blue meeting room
I stopped believing in sock liners and moulded footbeds.

I no longer believed in my boss though I still admired his arms—
the section from wrist to elbow—while talking lenticular logos.

At that particular moment by the photocopier I stopped
thinking about the Fall range and imagined thousands of shoes

travelling the world footloose and never coming in to land.
Even the lead designer—three slips of the tongue away

from calling me the *clueless marketing bitch* I clearly was—
on this day looked older and smaller and I forgot what time

zone I lived in, or how to spell my name. Somewhere between
the door of the blue meeting room, heavy with meaning—

form follows function —and the tubular chair, I stopped believing
in my hard-copy life, in cushioning, in adiprene™ and in everything

I'd learnt, or said, or done before that day. This had to stay secret.
I guarded it like a cat guards a bird with one wing: *mine, mine.*

Four star

I'm stuck to this spot like a leech drawing blood.
Half on a queen bed, half off.
Somewhere a foot hangs numb, a slab of thigh pocked by bed crumbs.
My foot, my thigh. Body parts as litter.
Playback time: a room service tray jiggles into shot. Pan out
to the remains of what we'd found in the minibar
smeared across surfaces or left to ooze where dropped.
All the messed-up contents of a crime scene
and on the wall some blur-faced peasants haul in the harvest,
sole reluctant witnesses to acts of swift undressing,
to the fiction of what gets said in the lingua franca of Marriotts & Hiltons.
Some kind of alarm beeps and pokes the blackout blind in my head.

In half an hour all this will be my history.
These sheets will be stripped, the last traces of me wheeled
to the service lift, like all the other cells I've shed
in all the four-star beds.
How short the way to this room, and hundreds like it.
How easy to mistake colleagues for lovers
hotels for havens
how familiar the ping of an elevator bell, the click of a plastic keycard
the soft sweep of a door across carpet
the sweetheart silence after closing.

1 Poultry

EC2R 8EJ

Shoot up in the fast lift,
poke the faux grass with toothpick heels.
Late lunch at the Coq d'Argent—
accept a drink, plan your exit.

After two pm the old religion can be smelt—
some urban Plague myth—even here,
halfway to the holding stacks
of City-bound planes.

Look out to where domes are clouds,
black antennas stricken trees, people
blips fading from someone's radar.
A good place to fail.

Tender is the man-made view.
Look down where a scrawl of red tail-lights
sings *stop in the name of love*
and windows laugh open.

One large Pinot Noir and all London
is under you, your parapet bends
eye-level with skinny cranes,
arms turning in a show of listening.

Eltham

You call it *that place where*
you label it like a curio, can't say
the name properly. Me and Kevin

at the bus stop down Well Hall
by Burtons, and over the road
I didn't see anything. Just

the church where cousin Joan
got hitched to a waster, back
in the forties. He went abroad,

we all did. Before the road cut
through the Corbett Estate—
the one with no pubs—Dunvegan

Road was halved, houses rubbed
out, with the library and Hind's
where we dropped sugar lumps

down the lift shaft, left to gurn
and lean over the crevasse, into
the new A2. The station kiosk gone.

I was asleep abroad, we all were.
Nobody saw what happened.
Me and Kevin at the bus stop.

He's dead now. And you label it
that place where—but where
is it for you? Where exactly?

London Bridge to Waterloo East

Ratcheted backwards along familiar lines
something is dead and we're the mourners—

a squeeze of tracks tight between windows
thirty bottle panes across, a *Pearce Duff's* sign,

shadow lines of a custard tin. Here we are
cheek to cheek with chimneys, eyelevel

with feral pigeons arranged like heraldry
in their smoke-blackened niches. Crane lower –

under a mash of adverts left to peeling, through
iron bars set in yellow brick, liquid escapes

down grilled steps, sensing the river. This fine
bent gristle thing nudges us into the old stories.

Our wheels sharpen on a drawn-out mass
of points and then we're stationary, our heaving

carriage balanced over Union Street arches,
hearts beating up out of sleeping bags below

where once packers and platers lit their fags,
off to the Rose & Crown, after the factory closed.

Performance

John Cage, 4'33" (1952)

He would staple a piano string to a cloud
in his empire of structured air—composer
of *play nothing, suspend everything,* the big unsung

serenade of O unravels. What do you hear?
Fricative chip of a cough, metallic snap stage left,
wet streets ribboned by tyre treads. Breaths

in the past tense, beyond useful. The 'happy birthday'
you sang over tequila shots in Bangkok
which I don't remember. Strangers crossing legs,

picking teeth. An age-old threat disguised as a cake.
A brace of whispers, an ice cream van—that smell.
I can't tell if I'm thinking out loud. There's a drill

at my temple, unhammering the outside world
into one tiny scratch as someone pushes back
their sleeve to reveal their watch, and wishes away

the awkward sounds of living. One unspoken *and*
hangs in an unreachable corner of the room
safe in the dust, needing no audience.

Is this the music we came here for? A piano grows old,
cars pass and people wait. Play nothing.
Suspend everything. Empty your head. Listen.

I am told I sing through my teeth

that my jaw is gridlocked
by some verbal blockage
even the dentist can't scrape off
the tartar of dead words
I must open my mouth more
my Scarlatti sonata is glottal stopped
get my tongue out of the way
or the palatals and labials will gather
unvoicing my Italian
making my gums bleed

I must open wide my maw
let the scales fly out
in daylight I sing through my teeth
at night I grind up words
if my tongue gets in the way
it yelps me awake
out of some lip-sync dream
I must stop biting down
on some imagined rope or hand
let *slack* be my last thought

I am told I should practise
in the bathroom mirror
check how many vowels I've stored
inside my wibbling mouth
swish and spit the same old tunes
all the flutey top notes I've never heard
are trapped and can't get out
there's nothing I can say to this
because my jaw is gridlocked
because my tongue is in the way

First Salsa in Cusco

Her T-shirt   was a shrug away   from shapeless   her head
was lost luggage   three thousand metres up   stuck
in the navel of the world   still   in her walking boots

and the sweat of the trek   who knows   if the taxi turned right
or left at the curl in the road   where someone left flowers
for the Black Madonna   said a prayer   and her llama face

there at the bar   among the vicuña women   up from Lima
up to the *altiplano*   watchful and gamine   on their delicate legs
if only   too many *pisco sours*—   and the music   subliminal

ceiling-high—   hadn't pulled her like a dropped note   into its drag
she might have left   before a city-boy   begged her dance
still   in her walking boots   before that Cinderella hoof

of hers was his   before she learned   to syn   copate
and curve with his body   allow herself to be moved   transfixed
by his CK1   or perhaps   a sudden tear-prick thought

of flowers by the road   or of home   and how far she might sink
or roll that night   deep as a silver mine   more precious
than old gold   *Just follow*   *like this:*   *left*   *right left*

Searching for the Police Tower, Orford Ness

By the rust road, a lattice strip of iron. Red-clad.
A dozen more, bent and furred between sea edge
and the Black Beacon: coils of crude traceries
discarded like mis-shapes. All objects wrestle
themselves in this easterly wind. The North Sea
heaves stones from their comfortable silence
up to the spit and the weathered calls of lapwings.

Once it was a humdrum of bombs. *Top Secret.*
We kick over an old binoculars case, another clue.
The Meccano tower is here on the map. Keep looking.
A concrete bunker's dark mouth breathes a whiff
of dereliction, down among the yellow poppies.
Something pathetic about the security gates, stuck
open and the fence gone. *Touch nothing suspicious.*

The police left in a hurry. Undercover barn owls,
in the eaves of Test Lab 5, wait for the ghosts
of scientists to magic saltpetre into freshwater.
What are we looking for, among the unexploded
ordnance? What is there left to find? Radio tower,
police tower, old business? Spat out onto shingle
with the rest, like every wreck that lost itself to water.

The summer we went to funerals

your suit smelt of floral tributes
and crematorium smoke - just one fag, you said
during *Sheep May Safely Graze.*

I learnt the importance of names—
Old Blush, Home Sweet Home—
fashioned into one big DAD
craning at the window of a hearse
holding up buses on the High Street.
You told me the cars must be immaculate.
All that glass. Respect is in the details.

I pictured Dad polishing his boots by the back door.
And later, his waxwork face framed in silk.

I came to recognise the rituals—
lads standing around awkward in black
old aunties looking for an arm
everyone waiting their turn in the sun.
Mourners fingering hymn books
not knowing the words, desperate for a drink.
The flower show as they left, cursory reading
of labels handwritten by strangers.
The chapel filling and emptying,
a ballcock priest bobbing on eddies of grief.

But you shut me out of the real business—
the night visits and all that happens
between a last breath and the first flames.
What winter really brings.
You said I wasn't ready for that.

Starry night

The constellation Pictor, named by Abbé Nicholas Louis de Lacaille in 1756

A bent line, not much more:
Pictor, the Abbé saw an easel
in you, twig-tendril afloat
in the Southern sky.

Your jaunty stance winks
neither canvas nor paint.
Three points pink, half-seen
from half the earth, your place

is mapped on a flat universe
that blindfolds us. And I
am further away from you
than the Abbé on a starry night,

or the artist whose mind
blended bright with black,
turned lines into swirls
flung colour at galaxies.

Two Honeymoons

1

One duff clutch on the Hardknott Pass,
one haunted cottage and a coalfire dead
on its knees, mud and more mud.

A photo shows me posing on a stile
in pink sweatpants, that curly perm,
a blurred expression. The miniature train

at Muncaster Castle, the hour's traffic jam
at Hawkshead, pubs full of climber blokes
up for Striding Edge. I don't recall the sex.

2

Now and then we left the third floor apartment
to fetch bread, or olives or a jar of ragù, to catch
a flash of a Plague Doctor's white beak crossing
from a blind alley, or a tethered gondola aloof
and rocking. A palazzo doorway was our heartland
and the city drew close, warmed its hands in ours.
We almost touched the prancing horses of St Mark's
from our window. Every night, in this church or that
we could have heard the *Four Seasons* by candlelight,
we talked of it but never went, and instead grew fat
on the silence of lapping water and our own mystery.
Winter was over and Spring sensed our impatience:
we didn't know how long we had, nor, if Venice
were to sink and send a thousand Titians out to sea
if we, naked and joyous as cherubim, would notice.